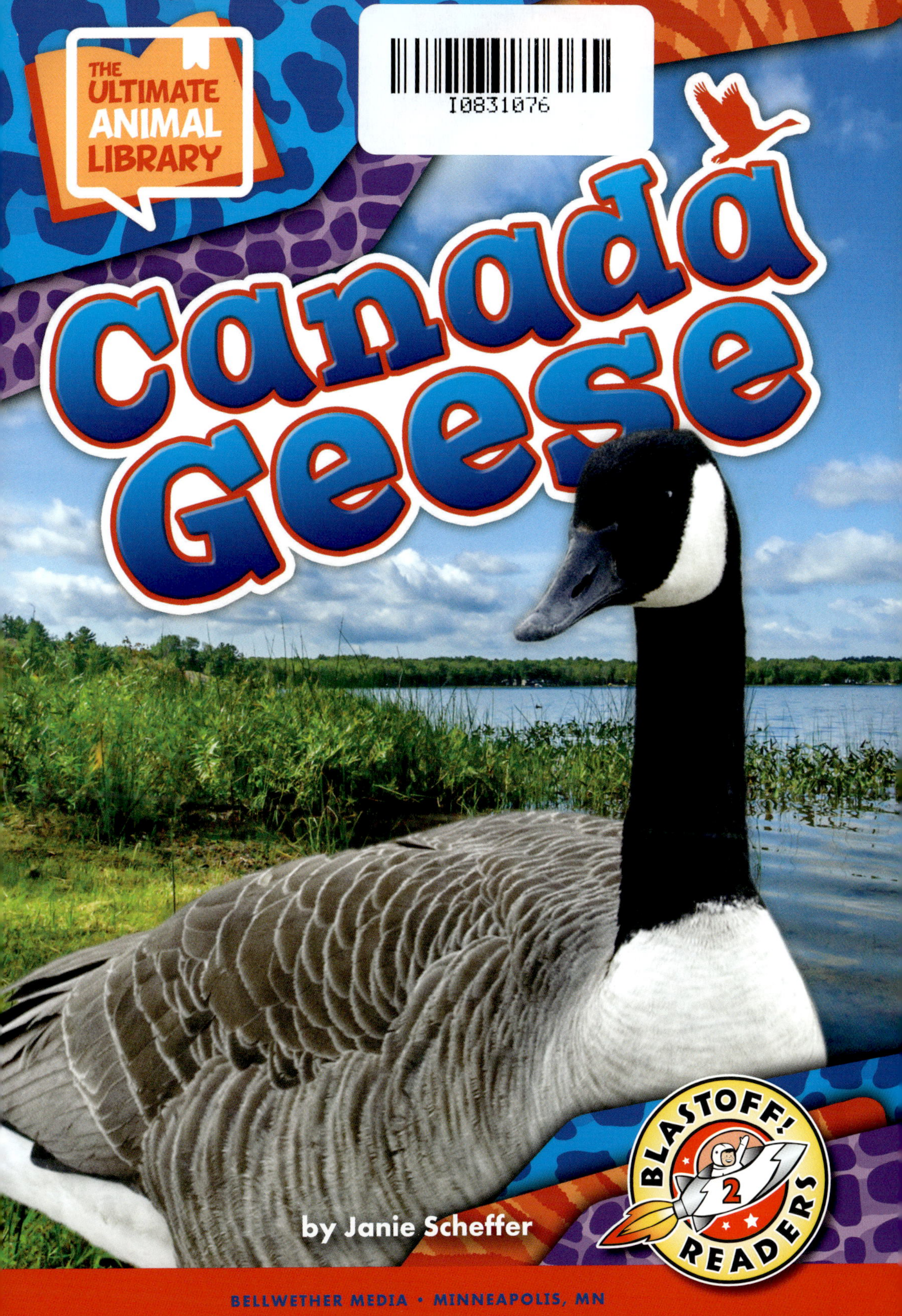

BELLWETHER MEDIA • MINNEAPOLIS, MN

Blastoff! Readers are carefully developed by literacy experts to build reading stamina and move students toward fluency by combining standards-based content with developmentally appropriate text.

Level 1 provides the most support through repetition of high-frequency words, light text, predictable sentence patterns, and strong visual support.

Level 2 offers early readers a bit more challenge through varied sentences, increased text load, and text-supportive special features.

Level 3 advances early-fluent readers toward fluency through increased text load, less reliance on photos, advancing concepts, longer sentences, and more complex special features.

★ **Blastoff! Universe**

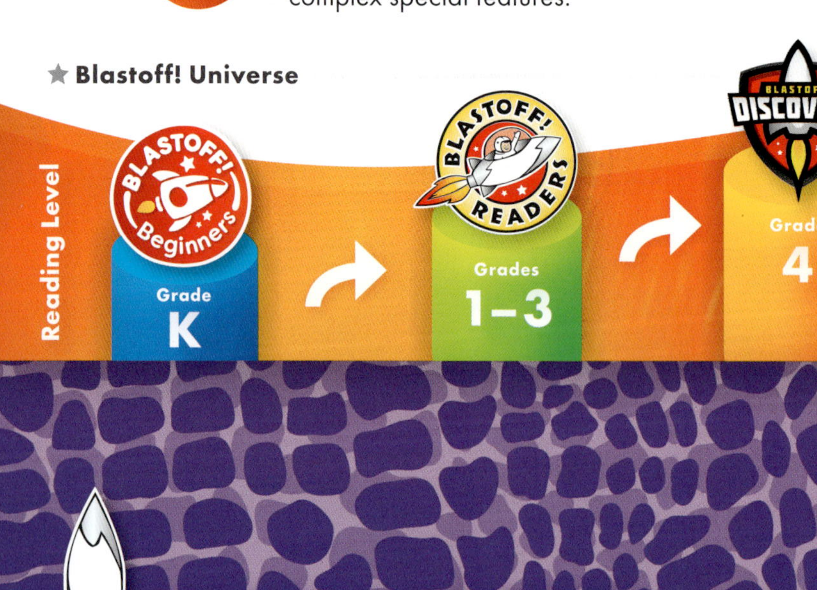

This edition first published in 2025 by Bellwether Media, Inc.

Library of Congress Cataloging-in-Publication Data

LC record for Canada Geese available at: https://lccn.loc.gov/2024012123

Editor: Elizabeth Neuenfeldt   Series Designer: Veah Demmin

Printed in the United States of America, North Mankato, MN.

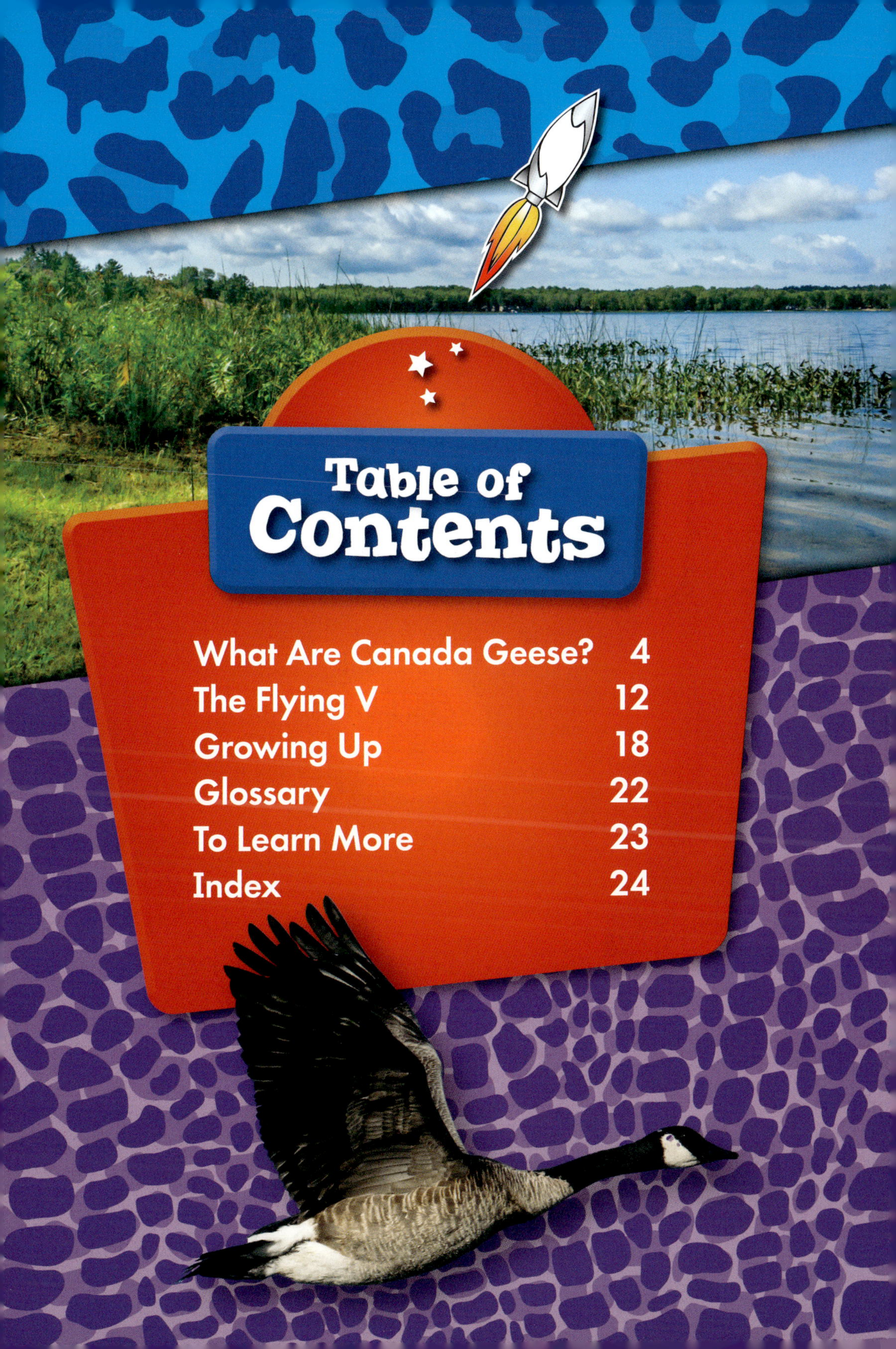

Table of Contents

What Are Canada Geese? 4
The Flying V 12
Growing Up 18
Glossary 22
To Learn More 23
Index 24

What Are Canada Geese?

Canada geese are loud birds. They are known for their honks! These geese mostly live in North America and Europe.

Canada Goose Report

Range

N
W E
S

range =

Status in the Wild

least concern

Habitats

grasslands

wetlands

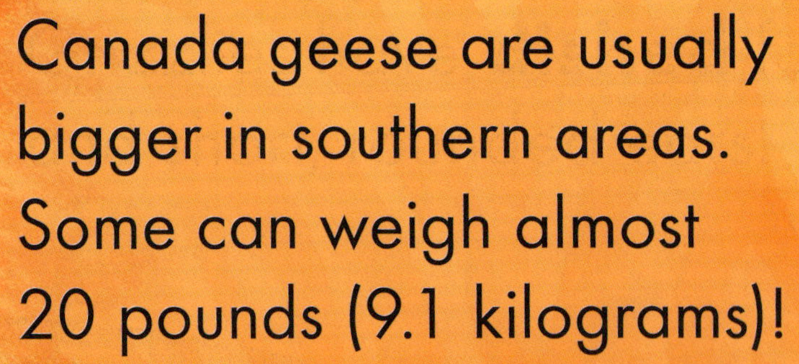

Canada geese are usually bigger in southern areas. Some can weigh almost 20 pounds (9.1 kilograms)!

Their **wingspans** can reach 5.6 feet (1.7 meters) wide.

Canada geese have black heads and long, black necks. Their cheeks and chins are white.

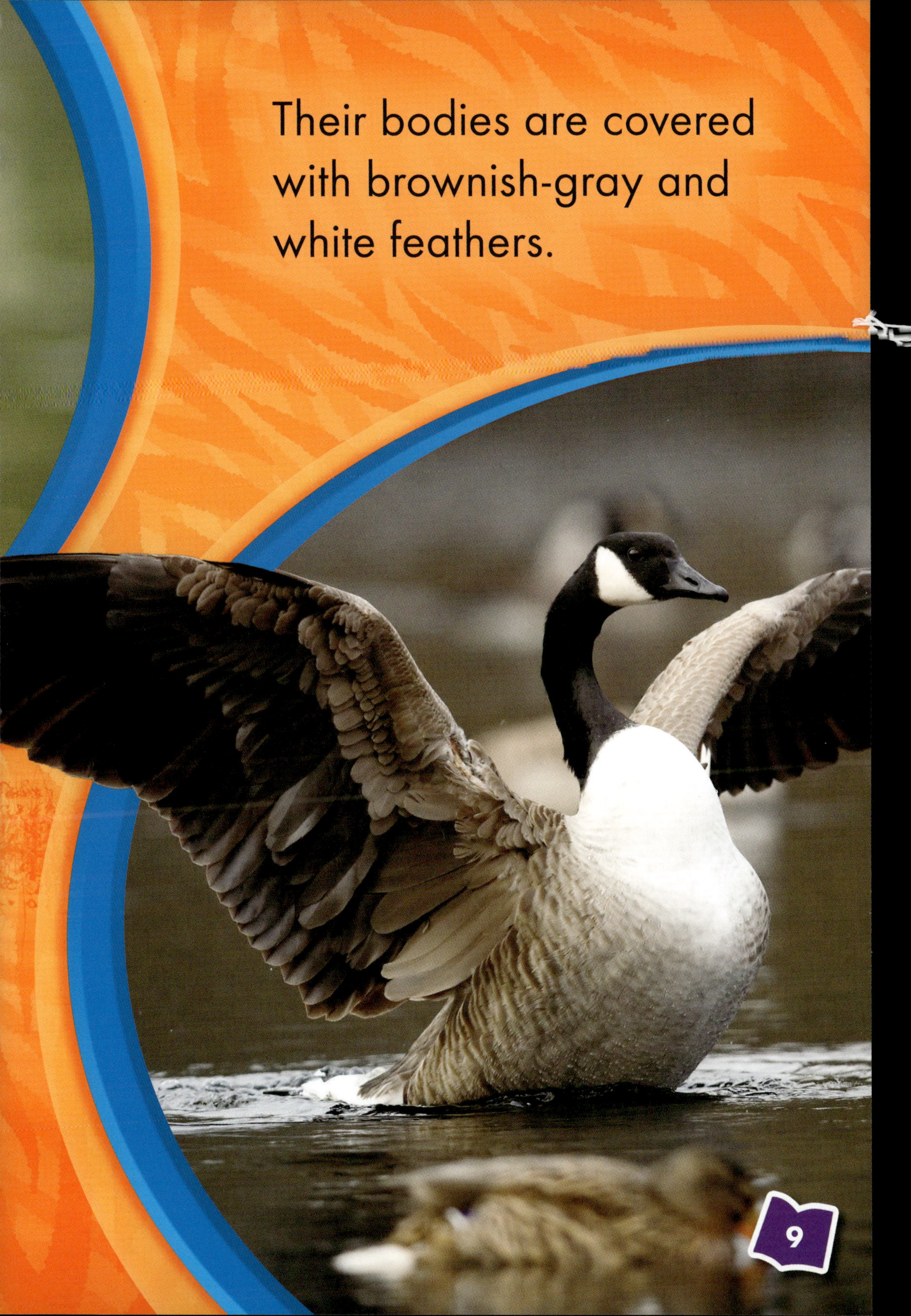

Their bodies are covered with brownish-gray and white feathers.

Canada geese have **webbed feet**. These help geese swim.

Canada geese have wide, flat **bills**. Their bills have toothlike points. These help geese eat.

Spot a Canada Goose

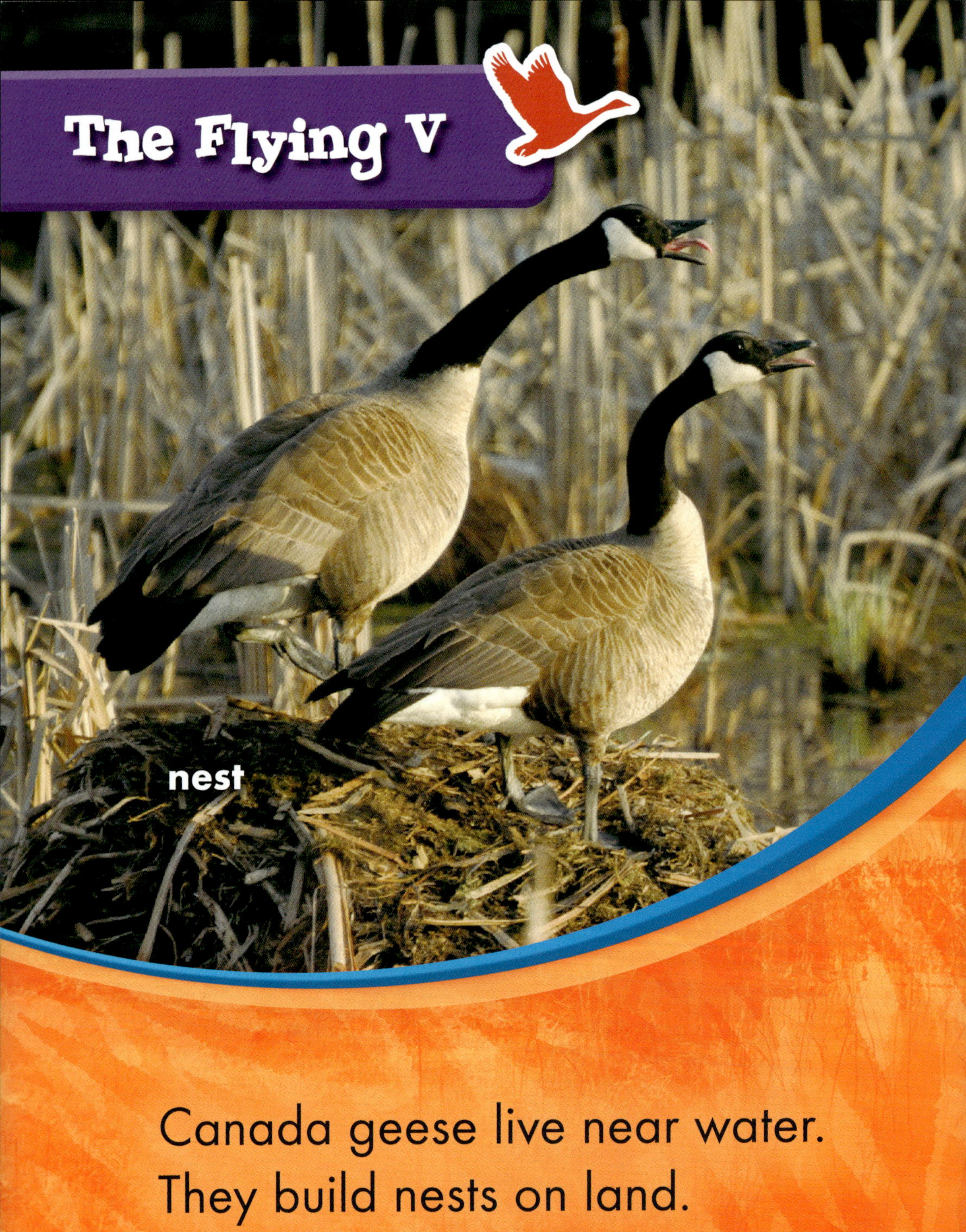

Canada geese live near water. They build nests on land.

These birds mostly live in big **flocks**. They honk to **communicate** and scare **predators**.

Canada geese are **herbivores**. They mostly eat plants.

They eat for about 12 hours each day. They spend more time eating before they **breed** or **migrate**!

In fall and spring, most Canada geese migrate. They fly in a V shape.

They travel up to 1,500 miles (2,414 kilometers) in a day!

Growing Up

Canada geese often **mate** for life. Females lay up to 11 eggs every spring.

The eggs **hatch** in around 28 days. **Goslings** walk and swim right away!

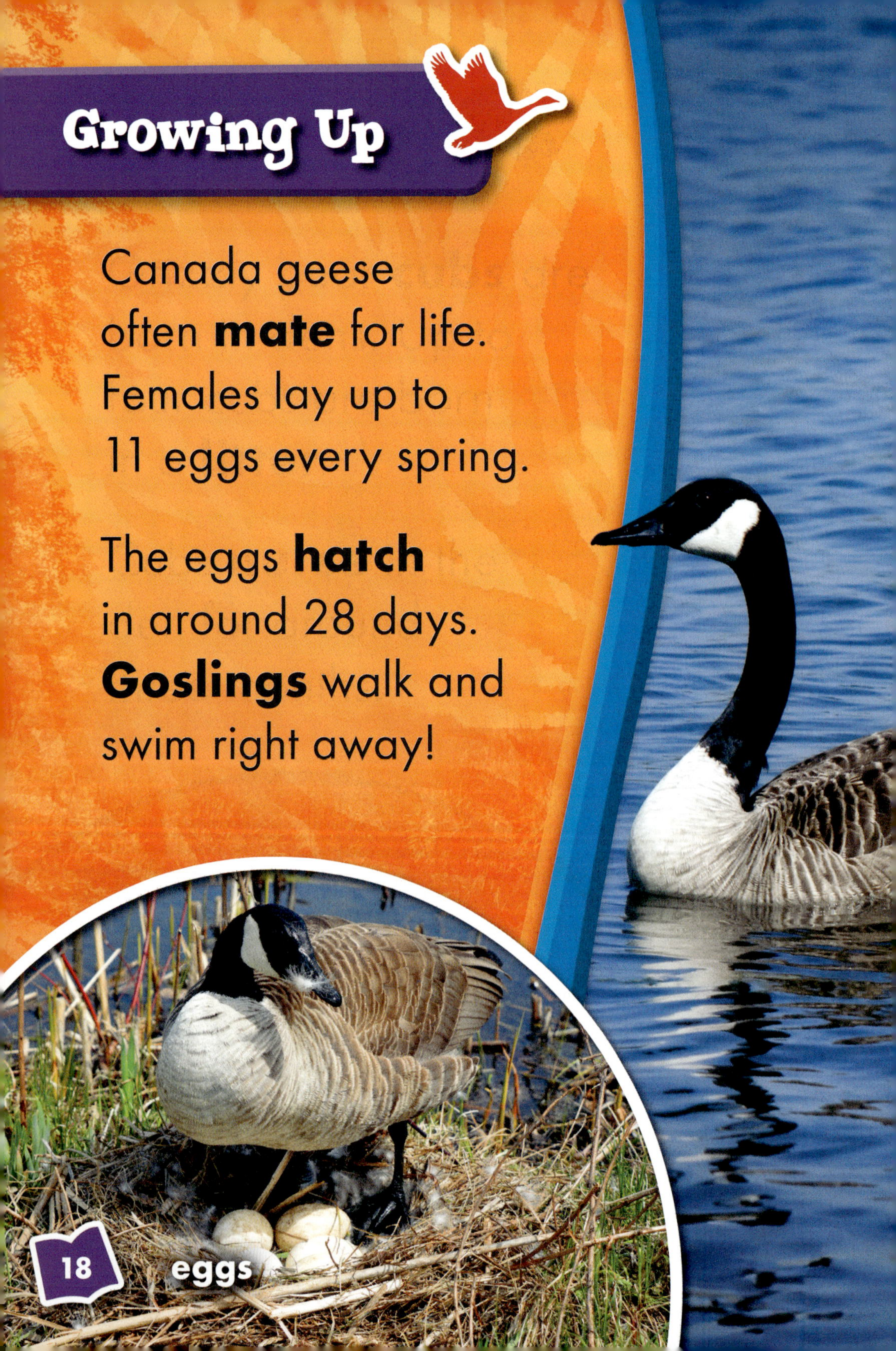

goslings

By nine weeks old,
goslings learn how to fly.

Goslings live with their parents for a year. Then they can live on their own!

Life of a Canada Goose

Name of Babies

goslings

Number of Eggs

up to 11

Time Spent in Egg

Life Span

Glossary

bills–the mouths of birds

breed–to produce young

communicate–to send and receive information

flocks–groups of birds

goslings–young geese

hatch–to break open

herbivores–animals that only eat plants

mate–to join together to make young

migrate–to travel from one place to another, often with the seasons

predators–animals that hunt other animals for food

webbed feet–feet with thin skin that connects the toes

wingspans–measurements of the distance from the tip of one wing to the tip of the other wing

To Learn More

AT THE LIBRARY

Hansen, Grace. *Canada Goose Migration.* Minneapolis, Minn.: Abdo Kids, 2021.

Rose, Rachel. *Goose Migration.* Minneapolis, Minn.: Bearport Publishing Company, 2024.

Sill, Cathryn P. *About Waterfowl: A Guide for Children.* Atlanta, Ga.: Peachtree Publishing Company, 2022.

ON THE WEB

FACTSURFER

Factsurfer.com gives you a safe, fun way to find more information.

1. Go to www.factsurfer.com.
2. Enter "Canada geese" into the search box and click 🔍.
3. Select your book cover to see a list of related content.

Index

bills, 10, 11
birds, 4, 13
bodies, 9
breed, 15
colors, 8, 9
communicate, 13
eat, 10, 14, 15
eggs, 18
Europe, 4
fall, 16
feathers, 9
females, 18
flocks, 13
fly, 16, 20
food, 14, 15
goslings, 18, 19, 20, 21
herbivores, 14
honks, 4, 13
life of a Canada goose, 21
mate, 18
migrate, 15, 16, 17
nests, 12
North America, 4
predators, 13
range, 4, 5
size, 6, 7
spot a Canada goose, 11
spring, 16, 18
status, 5
swim, 10, 18
walk, 18
water, 12
webbed feet, 10
wingspans, 7

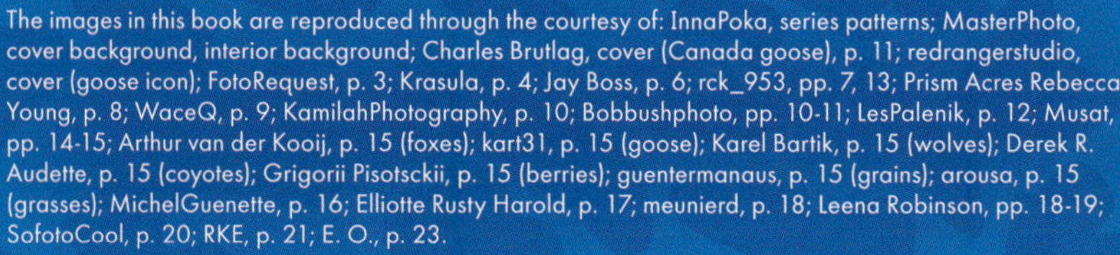

The images in this book are reproduced through the courtesy of: InnaPoka, series patterns; MasterPhoto, cover background, interior background; Charles Brutlag, cover (Canada goose), p. 11; redrangerstudio, cover (goose icon); FotoRequest, p. 3; Krasula, p. 4; Jay Boss, p. 6; rck_953, pp. 7, 13; Prism Acres Rebecca Young, p. 8; WaceQ, p. 9; KamilahPhotography, p. 10; Bobbushphoto, pp. 10-11; LesPalenik, p. 12; Musat, pp. 14-15; Arthur van der Kooij, p. 15 (foxes); kart31, p. 15 (goose); Karel Bartik, p. 15 (wolves); Derek R. Audette, p. 15 (coyotes); Grigorii Pisotsckii, p. 15 (berries); guentermanaus, p. 15 (grains); arousa, p. 15 (grasses); MichelGuenette, p. 16; Elliotte Rusty Harold, p. 17; meunierd, p. 18; Leena Robinson, pp. 18-19; SofotoCool, p. 20; RKE, p. 21; E. O., p. 23.